Fortinet Network Security
Architect

NSE 7

ENTERPRISE FIREWALL

**TOP-NOTCH QUESTIONS WITH COMPLETE
EXPLANATIONS AND REFERENCES**

Marilou Almoguera

Question #1

Examine the IPsec configuration shown in the exhibit; then answer the question below.

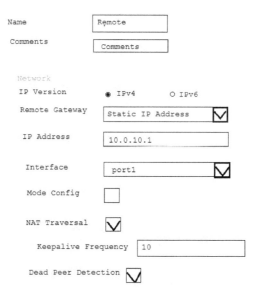

An administrator wants to monitor the VPN by enabling the IKE real time debug using these commands: diagnose vpn ike log-filter src-addr4 10.0.10.1 diagnose debug application ike -1 diagnose debug enable

The VPN is currently up, there is no traffic crossing the tunnel and DPD packets are being interchanged between both IPsec gateways. However, the IKE real time debug does NOT show any output. Why isn't there any output?

A. The IKE real time shows the phases 1 and 2 negotiations only. It does not show any more output once the tunnel is up.

B. The log-filter setting is set incorrectly. The VPN's traffic does not match this filter.

C. The IKE real time debug shows the phase 1 negotiation only. For information after that, the administrator must use the IPsec real time debug instead: diagnose debug application ipsec -1.

D. The IKE real time debug shows error messages only. If it does not provide any output, it indicates that the tunnel is operating normally.

Correct Answer: B

Question #2

Which of the following statements are true regarding the SIP session helper and the SIP application layer gateway (ALG)? (Choose three.)

A. SIP session helper runs in the kernel; SIP ALG runs as a user space process.

B. SIP ALG supports SIP HA failover; SIP helper does not.

C. SIP ALG supports SIP over IPv6; SIP helper does not.

D. SIP ALG can create expected sessions for media traffic; SIP helper does not.

E. SIP helper supports SIP over TCP and UDP; SIP ALG supports only SIP over UDP.

Correct Answer: ABC

Question #3

A FortiGate device has the following LDAP configuration:

```
config user ldap
    edit "WindowsLDAP"
      set server "10.0.1.10"
      set cnid "cn"
      set dn "cn=Users, dc=trainingAD, dc=training, dc=lab"
      set type regular
      set username "dc=trainingAD, dc=training, dc=lab"
      set password xxxxxxx
    next
end
```

The administrator executed the "~dsquery' command in the Windows LDAp server 10.0.1.10, and got the following output:

>dsquery user ""samid administrator

"CN=Administrator, CN=Users, DC=trainingAD, DC=training, DC=lab"

Based on the output, what FortiGate LDAP setting is configured incorrectly?

    A.   cnid.
    B.   username.
    C.   password.
    D.   dn.

Correct Answer: B

Question #4

Which of the following statements is true regarding a FortiGate configured as an explicit web proxy?

    A. FortiGate limits the number of simultaneous sessions per explicit web proxy user. This limit CANNOT be modified by the administrator.

    B. FortiGate limits the total number of simultaneous explicit web proxy users.

    C. FortiGate limits the number of simultaneous sessions per explicit web proxy user. The limit CAN be modified by the administrator.

    D. FortiGate limits the number of workstations that authenticate using the same web proxy user credentials. This limit CANNOT be modified by the administrator.

Correct Answer: B

Question #5

A corporate network allows Internet Access to FSSO users only. The FSSO user student does not have Internet access after successfully logged into the

Windows AD network. The output of the "˜diagnose debug authd fsso list' command does not show student as an active FSSO user. Other FSSO users can access the Internet without problems. What should the administrator check? (Choose two.)

A. The user student must not be listed in the CA's ignore user list.
B. The user student must belong to one or more of the monitored user groups.
C. The student workstation's IP subnet must be listed in the CA's trusted list.
D. At least one of the student's user groups must be allowed by a FortiGate firewall policy.

Correct Answer: AB

Question #6

An administrator has decreased all the TCP session timers to optimize the FortiGate memory usage. However, after the changes, one network application started to have problems. During the troubleshooting, the administrator noticed that the FortiGate deletes the sessions after the clients send the SYN packets, and before the arrival of the SYN/ACKs. When the SYN/ACK packets arrive to the FortiGate, the unit has already deleted the respective sessions. Which TCP session timer must be increased to fix this problem?

A. TCP half open.
B. TCP half close.
C. TCP time wait.
D. TCP session time to live.

Correct Answer: A

Question #7

An administrator is running the following sniffer in a FortiGate: diagnose sniffer packet any "host 10.0.2.10" 2

What information is included in the output of the sniffer? (Choose two.)

    A. Ethernet headers.
    B. IP payload.
    C. IP headers.
    D. Port names.

Correct Answer: BC

Question #8

Examine the partial output from two web filter debug commands; then answer the question below:

```
# diagnose test application urlfilter 3
Domain | IP    DB Ver   T URL
34000000| 34000000   16.40224 P Bhttp://www.fgt99.com/
# get webfilter categories
g07 General Interest - Business:
     34 Finance and Banking
     37 Search Engines and Portals
     43 General Organizations
     49 Business
     50 Information and Computer Security
     51 Government and Legal Organizations
     52 Information Technology
```

Based on the above outputs, which is the FortiGuard web filter category for the web site www.fgt99.com?

A. Finance and banking

B. General organization.

C. Business.

D. Information technology.

Correct Answer: D

Question #9

Examine the output of the "~get router info ospf interface' command shown in the exhibit; then answer the question below.

```
# get router info ospf interface port4
port4 is up, line protocol is up
    Internet Address 172.20.121.236/24, Area 0.0.0.0, MTU 1500
    Process ID 0, Router ID 0.0.0.4, Network Type BROADCAST, Cost: 1
    Transmit Delay is 1 sec, State DROther, Priority 1
    Designated Router (ID) 172.20.140.2, Interface Address 172.20.121.2
Backup Designated Router (ID) 0.0.0.1, Interface Address
172.20.121.239
Timer intervals configured, Hello 10.000, Dead 40, Wait 40, Retransmit
5
     Hello due in 00:00:05
    Neighbor Count is 4, Adjacent neighbor count is 2
    Crypt Sequence Number is 411
    Hello received 106, sent 27, DD received 7 sent 9
    LS-Req received 2 sent 2, LS-Upd received 7 sent 5
    LS-Ack received 4 sent 3, Discarded 1
```

Which statements are true regarding the above output? (Choose two.)

A. The port4 interface is connected to the OSPF backbone area.

B. The local FortiGate has been elected as the OSPF backup designated router.

C. There are at least 5 OSPF routers connected to the port4 network.

D. Two OSPF routers are down in the port4 network.

Correct Answer: AC

Question #10

Examine the output of the "˜get router info bgp summary' command shown in the exhibit; then answer the question below.

```
# get router info bgp summary
BGP router identifier 0.0.0.117, local AS number 65117
BGP table version is 104
3 BGP AS-PATH entries
0 BGP community entries

Neighbor       V    AS   MsgRcvd  MsgSent  TblVer  InQ  OutQ  Up/Down   State/PfxRcd
10.125.0.60    4  65060  1698     1756     103     0    0     03:02:49         1
10.127.0.75    4  65075  2206     2250     102     0    0     02:45:55         1
10.200.3.1     4  65501  101      115      0       0    0     never      Active

Total number of neighbors 3
```

Which statements are true regarding the output in the exhibit? (Choose two.)

A. BGP state of the peer 10.125.0.60 is Established.

B. BGP peer 10.200.3.1 has never been down since the BGP counters were cleared.

C. Local BGP peer has not received an OpenConfirm from 10.200.3.1.

D. The local BGP peer has received a total of 3 BGP prefixes.

Correct Answer: AC

Question #11

Examine the following partial output from a sniffer command; then answer the question below.

```
# diagnose sniff packet any 'icmp' 4
interfaces= [any]
filters = [icmp]
2.101199 wan2 in 192.168.1.110-> 4.2.2.2: icmp: echo request
2.101400 wan1 out 172.17.87.16-> 4.2.2.2: icmp: echo request
......
2.123500 wan2 out 4.2.2.2-> 192.168.1.110: icmp: echo reply
244 packets received by filter
5 packets dropped by kernel
```

What is the meaning of the packets dropped counter at the end of the sniffer?

    A.   Number of packets that didn't match the sniffer filter.

    B.   Number of total packets dropped by the FortiGate.

    C.   Number of packets that matched the sniffer filter and were dropped by the FortiGate.

    D.   Number of packets that matched the sniffer filter but could not be captured by the sniffer.

Correct Answer: D

Question #12

A FortiGate is configured as an explicit web proxy. Clients using this web proxy are reposting DNS errors when accessing any website. The administrator executes the following debug commands and observes that the n-dns-timeout counter is increasing:

```
#diagnose test application wad 2200
#diagnose test application wad 104
DNS Stats:
n_dns_reqs=878   n_dns_fails= 2   n_dns_timeout=875
n_dns_success=0

n_snd_retries=0   n_snd_fails=0 n_snd_success=0 n_dns_overflow=0
n_build_fails=0
```

What should the administrator check to fix the problem?

    A. The connectivity between the FortiGate unit and the DNS server.

    B. The connectivity between the client workstations and the DNS server.

    C. That DNS traffic from client workstations is allowed by the explicit web proxy policies.

    D. That DNS service is enabled in the explicit web proxy interface.

Correct Answer: AB

Question #13

Which real time debug should an administrator enable to troubleshoot RADIUS authentication problems?

    A. Diagnose debug application radius -1.
    B. Diagnose debug application fnbamd -1.
    C. Diagnose authd console ""log enable.
    D. Diagnose radius console ""log enable.

Correct Answer: B

Question #14

Examine the output of the "~diagnose sys session list expectation' command shown in the exhibit; than answer the question below.

```
#diagnose sys session list expectation

session info: proto= proto_state=0 0 duration=3 expire=26 timeout=3600
flags=00000000
sockflag= ·00000000 ·sockport=0 ·av_idx=0 ·use=3¶
origin-shaper=¶
reply-shaper=¶
per-ip_shaper=¶
ha_id=0 ·policy_dir=1 ·tunnel=/¶
state=new complex
statistic (bytes/packets/allow_err): org=0/0/0 reply=0/0/0 tuples=2
orgin-> sink: org pre-> post, reply pre->post dev=2->4/4->2
gwy=10.0.1.10/10.200.1.254
hook=pre dir=org act=dnat 10.171.121.38:0-> 10.200.1.1: 60426
(10.0.1.10: 50365)¶
hook= pre dir=org act=noop 0.0.0.0.:0-> 0.0.0.0:0 (0.0.0.0:0)
pos/(before, after) 0/(0,0), 0/(0,0)
misc=0 ·policy_id=1 ·auth_info=0 ·chk_client_info=0 ·vd=0
serial1=000000e9 ·tos=ff/ff ·ips_view=0 app_list=0 ·app=0
dd type=0 ·dd_mode=0¶
```

Which statement is true regarding the session in the exhibit?

- A. It was created by the FortiGate kernel to allow push updates from FotiGuard.
- B. It is for management traffic terminating at the FortiGate.
- C. It is for traffic originated from the FortiGate.
- D. It was created by a session helper or ALG.

Correct Answer: D

Question #15

An administrator has configured a FortiGate device with two VDOMs: root and internal. The administrator has also created and inter-VDOM link that connects both

VDOMs. The objective is to have each VDOM advertise some routes to the other VDOM via OSPF through the inter-VDOM link. What OSPF configuration settings must match in both VDOMs to have the OSPF adjacency successfully forming? (Choose three.)

- A. Router ID.
- B. OSPF interface area.
- C. OSPF interface cost.
- D. OSPF interface MTU.
- E. Interface subnet mask.

Correct Answer: BDE

Question #16

An administrator has configured a dial-up IPsec VPN with one phase 2, extended authentication (XAuth) and IKE mode configuration. The administrator has also enabled the IKE real time debug: diagnose debug application ike-1 diagnose debug enable

In which order is each step and phase displayed in the debug output each time a new dial-up user is connecting to the VPN?

- A. Phase1; IKE mode configuration; XAuth; phase 2.
- B. Phase1; XAuth; IKE mode configuration; phase2.
- C. Phase1; XAuth; phase 2; IKE mode configuration.
- D. Phase1; IKE mode configuration; phase 2; XAuth.

Correct Answer: B

Question #17

Two independent FortiGate HA clusters are connected to the same broadcast domain. The administrator has reported that both clusters are using the same HA virtual MAC address. This creates a duplicated MAC address problem in the network. What HA setting must be changed in one of the HA clusters to fix the problem?

- A. Group ID.
- B. Group name.
- C. Session pickup.
- D. Gratuitous ARPs.

Correct Answer: A

Question #18

When does a RADIUS server send an Access-Challenge packet?

    A. The server does not have the user credentials yet.
    B. The server requires more information from the user, such as
        the token code for two-factor authentication.
    C. The user credentials are wrong.
    D. The user account is not found in the server.

Correct Answer: B

Question #19

The logs in a FSSO collector agent (CA) are showing the following
error: failed to connect to registry: PIKA1026 (192.168.12.232)

What can be the reason for this error?

    A. The CA cannot resolve the name of the workstation.
    B. The FortiGate cannot resolve the name of the workstation.
    C. The remote registry service is not running in the workstation
        192.168.12.232.
    D. The CA cannot reach the FortiGate with the IP address
        192.168.12.232.

Correct Answer: C

Question #20

Examine the output of the "˜get router info ospf neighbor' command shown in the exhibit; then answer the question below.

```
# get router info ospf neighbor

OSPF process 0:
Neighbor ID   Pri   State          Dead Time   Address        Interface
0.0.0.69       1    Full/DR        00:00:32    10.126.0.69    wan1
0.0.0.117      1    Full/DROther   00:00:34    10.126.0.117   wan1
0.0.0.2        1    Full/ -        00:00:36    172.16.1.2     ToRemote
```

Which statements are true regarding the output in the exhibit? (Choose two.)

    A. The interface ToRemote is OSPF network type point-to-point.

    B. The OSPF router with the ID 0.0.0.2 is the designated router for the ToRemote network.

    C. The local FortiGate is the backup designated router for the wan1 network.

    D. The OSPF routers with the IDs 0.0.0.69 and 0.0.0.117 are both designated routers for the wan1 network.

Correct Answer: AC

Question #21

A FortiGate has two default routes:

```
config router static
   edit 1
      set gateway 10.200.1.254
      set priority 5
      set device "port1"
   next
   edit2
      set gateway 10.200.2.254
      set priority 10
      set device "port2"
   next
end
```

All Internet traffic is currently using port1. The exhibit shows partial information for one sample session of Internet traffic from an internal user:

```
# diagnose sys session list
Session info: proto=6 proto_state=01 duration =17 expire=7 timeout=3600
flags= 00000000 sockflag=00000000 sockport=0 av idx=0 use=3
ha_id=0 policy_dir=0 tunnel=/
state=may_dirty none app_ntf
statistic (bytes/packets/allow_err): org=575/7/1 reply=23367/19/1 tuples=2
origin->sink: org pre->post, reply pre->post dev=4->2/2->4
gwy=10.200.1.254/10.0.1.10
hook=post dir=org act=snat 10.0.1.10:64907-
>54.239.158.170:80(10.200.1.1:64907)
hook=pre ·dir=reply act=dnat 54.239.158.170:80-
>10.200.1.1:64907(10.0.1.10:64907)
pos/(before, after) 0/(0,0), 0/(0,0)
misc=0 policy_id=1 auth_info=0 chk_client_info=0 vd=0
serial=00000294 tos=ff/ff ips_view=0 app_list=0 app=0
dd_type=0 dd_mode=0
```

What would happen with the traffic matching the above session if the priority on the first default route (IDd1) were changed from 5 to 20?

- A. Session would remain in the session table and its traffic would keep using port1 as the outgoing interface.
- B. Session would remain in the session table and its traffic would start using port2 as the outgoing interface.

16

C. Session would be deleted, so the client would need to start a new session.

D. Session would remain in the session table and its traffic would be shared between port1 and port2.

Correct Answer: A

Question #22

What events are recorded in the crashlogs of a FortiGate device? (Choose two.)

A. A process crash.
B. Configuration changes.
C. Changes in the status of any of the FortiGuard licenses.
D. System entering to and leaving from the proxy conserve mode.

Correct Answer: AD

Question #23

Examine the following partial outputs from two routing debug commands; then answer the question below:

```
#get router info routing-table database
S     0.0.0.0/. [20/0] via 10.200.2.254, port2, [10/0]
S     *> 0.0.0.0/0 [10/0] via 10.200.1.254, port1
# get router info routing-table all
S*    0.0.0.0/0 [10/0] via 10.200.1.254, port1
```

Why the default route using port2 is not displayed in the output of the second command?

    A.   It has a lower priority than the default route using port1.
    B.   It has a higher priority than the default route using port1.
    C.   It has a higher distance than the default route using port1.
    D.   It is disabled in the FortiGate configuration.

Correct Answer: C

Question #24

A FortiGate is rebooting unexpectedly without any apparent reason. What troubleshooting tools could an administrator use to get more information about the problem? (Choose two.)

    A.   Firewall monitor.
    B.   Policy monitor.
    C.   Logs.
    D.   Crashlogs.

Correct Answer: CD

Question #25

An administrator has enabled HA session synchronization in a HA cluster with two members. Which flag is added to a primary unit's session to indicate that it has been synchronized to the secondary unit?

- A. redir.
- B. dirty.
- C. synced
- D. nds.

Correct Answer: C

Question #26

Examine the output of the "˜get router info bgp summary' command shown in the exhibit; then answer the question below.

```
Student# get router info bgp summary
BGP router indentifier 10.200.1.1, local AS number 65500
BGP table version is 2
1 BGP AS-PATH entries
0 BGP community entries

Neighbor  V    AS   MsgRcvd MsgSent TblVer InQ OutQ Up/Down State/PfxRcd
10.200.3.1 4  65501     92     112     0    0    0    never   Connect

Total number of neighbors 1
```

Which statement can explain why the state of the remote BGP peer 10.200.3.1 is Connect?

- A. The local peer is receiving the BGP keepalives from the remote peer but it has not received any BGP prefix yet.

19

B. The TCP session for the BGP connection to 10.200.3.1 is down.

C. The local peer has received the BGP prefixed from the remote peer.

D. The local peer is receiving the BGP keepalives from the remote peer but it has not received the OpenConfirm yet.

Correct Answer: B

Question #27

Examine the output of the "˜diagnose ips anomaly list' command shown in the exhibit; then answer the question below.

```
# diagnose ips anomaly list

list nids meter:
id=ip_dst_session      ip=192.168.1.10    dos_id=2  exp=3646  pps=0  freq=0
id=udp_dst_session     ip=192.168.1.10    dos_id=2  exp=3646  pps=0  freq=0
id=udp_scan            ip=192.168.1.110   dos_id=1  exp=649   pps=0  freq=0
id=udp_flood           ip=192.168.1.110   dos_id=2  exp=653   pps=0  freq=0
id=tcp_src_session     ip=192.168.1.110   dos_id=1  exp=5175  pps=0  freq=8
id=tcp_port_scan       ip=192.168.1.110   dos_id=1  exp=175   pps=0  freq=0
id=ip_src_session      ip=192.168.1.110   dos_id=1  exp=5649  pps=0  freq=30
id=udp_src_session     ip=192.168.1.110   dos_id=1  exp=5649  pps=0  freq=22
```

Which IP addresses are included in the output of this command?

A. Those whose traffic matches a DoS policy.

B. Those whose traffic matches an IPS sensor.

C. Those whose traffic exceeded a threshold of a matching DoS policy.

D. Those whose traffic was detected as an anomaly by an IPS sensor.

Correct Answer: A

Question #28

Examine the partial output from the IKE real time debug shown in the exhibit; then answer the question below.

```
#diagnose debug application ike -1
#diagnose debug enable
ike 0: .....: 75: responder: aggressive mode get 1st message…
…
ike 0: ....:76: incoming proposal:
ike 0: ....:76: proposal id = 0:
ike 0: ....:76:   protocol id= ISAKMP:
ike 0: ....:76:     trans_id = KEY_IKE.
ike 0: ....:76:     encapsulation = IKE/none
ike 0: ....:76:       type= OAKLEY_ENCRYPT_ALG, val=AES_CBC.
ike 0: ....:76:       type= OAKLEY_HASH_ALG, val=SHA2_256.
ike 0: ....:76:       type=AUTH_METHOD, val=PRESHARED_KEY.
ike 0: ....:76:       type=OAKLEY_GROUP, val=MODP2048.
ike 0: ....:76: ISAKMP SA lifetime=86400
ike 0: ....:76: my proposal, gw Remote:
ike 0: ....:76: proposal id=1:
ike 0: ....:76:   protocol id= ISAKMP:
ike 0: ....:76:     trans_id= KEY_IKE.
ike 0: ....:76:     encapsulation = IKE/none
ike 0: ....:76:       type=OAKLEY_ECNRYPT_ALG, val=DES_CBC.
ike 0: ....:76:       type=OAKLEY_HASH_ALG, val=SHA2_256.
ike 0: ....:76:       type=AUTH_METHOD, val= PRESHARED_KEY.
ike 0: ....:76:       type=OAKLEY_GROUP, val =MODP2048.
ike 0: ....:76: ISAKMP SA lifetime=86400
ike 0: ....:76: proposal id=1:
ike 0: ....:76:   protocol id= ISAKMP:
ike 0: ....:76:     trans_id= KEY_IKE.
ike 0: ....:76:     encapsulation = IKE/none
ike 0: ....:76:       type=OAKLEY_ENCRYPT_ALG, val=DES_CBC.
ike 0: ....:76:       type= OAKLEY_HASH_ALG, val=SHA2_256.
```

Why didn't the tunnel come up?

- A. IKE mode configuration is not enabled in the remote IPsec gateway.
- B. The remote gateway's Phase-2 configuration does not match the local gateway's phase-2 configuration.
- C. The remote gateway's Phase-1 configuration does not match the local gateway's phase-1 configuration.
- D. One IPsec gateway is using main mode, while the other IPsec gateway is using aggressive mode.

Correct Answer: C

Question #29

A FortiGate device has the following LDAP configuration:

```
config user ldap
    edit "WindowsLDAP"
      set server "10.0.1.10"
      set cnid "cn"
      set dn "cn=user, dc=trainingAD, dc=training, dc=lab"
      set type regular
      set username "cn=administrator, cn=users, dc=trainingAD,
dc=training, dc=lab"
      set password xxxxx
    next
end
```

The LDAP user student cannot authenticate. The exhibit shows the output of the authentication real time debug while testing the student account:

```
#diagnose debug application fnbamd -1
#diagnose debug enable
#diagnose test authserver ldap WindowsLDAP student password
fnbamd_fsm.c[1819] handle_req-Rcvd auth req 4 for student in WindowsLDAP
opt=27 prot=0
fnbamd_fsm.c[336]_compose _group_list_from_req_Group 'WindowsLDAP'
fnbamd_pop3.c[573] fnband_pop3_start-student
fnbamd_cfg.c[932] fnbamd_cfg-get_ldap_;ist_by_server-Loading LDAP server
'WindowsLDAP'
fnbamd_ldap.c[992] resolve_ldap_FQDN-Resolved address 10.0.1.10, result 10.0.1.10
fnbamd_fsm.c[428] create_ auth_session-Total 1 server (s) to try
fnbamd_ldap.c[1700] fnbamd_ldap_get_result-Error in ldap result: 49
(Invalid credentials)
fnbamd_ldap.c[2028] fnbamd_ldap_get_result-Auth denied
fnbamd_auth.c[2188] fnbamd_auth_poll_ldap-Result for ldap svr 10.0.1.10 is denied
fnbamd_comm.c[169] fnbamd_comm_send_result-Sending result 1 for req 4
fnbamd_fsm.c[568] destroy_auth_session-delete session 4
authenticate 'student' against 'WindowsLDAP' failed!
```

Based on the above output, what FortiGate LDAP settings must the administer check? (Choose two.)

    A.   cnid.

    B.   username.

    C.   password.

    D.   dn.

Correct Answer: BC

Question #30

Examine the output from the "~diagnose vpn tunnel list' command shown in the exhibit; then answer the question below.

```
#diagnose vpn tunnel list
name-Dial Up_0 ver=1 serial=5 10.200.1.1:4500->10.200.3.2: 64916 lgwy=static
nun=intf mode=dial_inst.bound if=2
parent=DialUp index=0
proxyid_um=1 child_num=0 refcnt=8 ilast=4 olast=4
stat: rxp=104 txp=8 rxb=27392 txb=480
dpd: mode=active on=1 idle=5000ms retry=3 count=0 segno=70
natt: mode=silent draft=32 interval= 10 remote_port=64916
proxyid= DialUp proto=0 sa=1 ref=2 serial=1 add-route
  src: 0:0.0.0.0.-255.255.255.255:0
  dst: 0:10.0.10.10.-10.0.10.10:0
  SA: ref=3 options= 00000086 type=00 soft=0 mtu=1422 expire =42521
replaywin=2048 seqno=9
  life: type=01 bytes=0/0 timeout= 43185/43200
  dec: spi=cb3a632a esp=aes key=16  7365e17a8fd555ec38bffa47d650c1a2
       ah=sha1 key=20  946bfb9d23b8b53770dcf48ac2af82b8ccc6aa85
  enc: spi=da6d28ac esp=aes key=16  3dcf44ac7c816782ea3d0c9a977ef543
       ah=sha1 key=20  7cfde587592fc4635ab8db8ddf0d851d868b243f
dec:pkts/bytes=104/19926, enc:pkts/bytes=8/1024
```

Which command can be used to sniffer the ESP traffic for the VPN
DialUP_0?

    A.   diagnose sniffer packet any "~port 500'

    B.   diagnose sniffer packet any "~esp'

    C.   diagnose sniffer packet any "~host 10.0.10.10'

    D.   diagnose sniffer packet any "~port 4500'

Correct Answer: D

Question #31

View the central management configuration shown in the exhibit, and
then answer the question below.

```
config system central-management
    set type fortimanager
    set fmg "10.0.1.242"
    config server-list
        edit 1
            set server-type rating
            set server-address 10.0.1.240
        next
        edit 2
            set server-type update
            set server-address 10.0.1.243
        next
        edit 3
            set server-type rating
            set server-address 10.0.1.244
        next
    end
    set include-default-servers enable
end
```

Which server will FortiGate choose for antivirus and IPS updates

if 10.0.1.243 is experiencing an outage?

- A. 10.0.1.240
- B. One of the public FortiGuard distribution servers
- C. 10.0.1.244
- D. 10.0.1.242

Correct Answer: B

Question #32

View the exhibit, which contains the output of diagnose sys session stat, and then answer the question below.

```
NGFW-1 # diagnose sys session stat
misc info:      session_count=591  setup_rate=0  exp_count=0
clash=162  memory_tension_drop=0  ephemeral=0/65536
removeable=0
delete=0, flush-0, dev_down=0/0
TCP sessions:
        166 in NONE state
        1 in ESTABLISHED state
        3 in SYN_SENT state
        2 in TIME_WAIT state
firewall error stat:
error1=00000000
error2=00000000
error3=00000000
error4=00000000
tt=00000000
cont=00000000
ids_recv=00000000
url_recv=00000000
av_recv=00000000
fqdn_count=00000006
global: ses_limit=0  ses6_limit=0  rt_limit=0  rt6_limit=0
```

Which statements are correct regarding the output shown? (Choose two.)

    A. There are 0 ephemeral sessions.
    B. All the sessions in the session table are TCP sessions.
    C. No sessions have been deleted because of memory pages exhaustion.
    D. There are 166 TCP sessions waiting to complete the three-way handshake.

Correct Answer: AC

Question #33

View the exhibit, which contains the output of a debug command, and then answer the question below.

```
#dia hardware sysinfo shm
SHM counter:              150
SHM allocated:              0
SHM total:        625057792
conserve mode: on - mem
system last entered: Mon Apr 24 16:36:37 2017
sys fd last entered: n/a
SHM FS total:   641236992
SHM FS free:    641208320
SHM FS avail:   641208320
SHM FS alloc:       28672
```

What statement is correct about this FortiGate?

    A.   It is currently in system conserve mode because of high CPU usage.

    B.   It is currently in FD conserve mode.

    C.   It is currently in kernel conserve mode because of high memory usage.

    D.   It is currently in system conserve mode because of high memory usage.

Correct Answer: D

Question #34

Which statements about bulk configuration changes using FortiManager CLI scripts are correct? (Choose two.)

- A. When executed on the Policy Package, ADOM database, changes are applied directly to the managed FortiGate.
- B. When executed on the Device Database, you must use the installation wizard to apply the changes to the managed FortiGate.
- C. When executed on the All FortiGate in ADOM, changes are automatically installed without creating a new revision history.
- D. When executed on the Remote FortiGate directly, administrators do not have the option to review the changes prior to installation.

Correct Answer: BD

Question #35

Which of the following tasks are automated using the Install Wizard on FortiManager? (Choose two.)

- A. Preview pending configuration changes for managed devices.
- B. Add devices to FortiManager.
- C. Import policy packages from managed devices.
- D. Install configuration changes to managed devices.
- E. Import interface mappings from managed devices.

Correct Answer: AD

Question #36

View the exhibit, which contains the output of diagnose sys session list, and then answer the question below.

```
# diagnose sys session list
session info: proto=6 proto_state=01 duration=73 expire=3597 timeout=3600
flags=00000000 sockflag=00000000 sockport=0 av_idx=0 use=3
origin-shaper=
reply-shaper=
per_ip_shaper=
ha_id=0 policy_dir=0 tunnel=/
state=may_dirty synced none app_ntf
statistic (bytes/packets/allow_err): org=822/11/1 reply=9037/15/1 tuples=2
orgin->sink: org pre->post, reply pre->post dev=4->2/2->4 gwy=10.200.1.254/10.0.1.10
hook=post dir=org act=snat 10.0.1.10:65464->54.192.15.182:80(10.200.1.1:65464)
hook-pre dir=reply act=dnat 54.192.15.182:80->10.200.1.1:65464(10.0.1.10:65464)
pos/ (before, after) 0/(0/0), 0/(0,0)
misc=0 policy_id=1 auth_info=0 chk_client_info=0 vd=0
serial=00000098 tos=ff/ff ips_view=0 app_list=0 app=0
dd_type=0 dd_mode=0
```

If the HA ID for the primary unit is zero (0), which statement is correct regarding the output?

- A. This session is for HA heartbeat traffic.
- B. This session is synced with the slave unit.
- C. The inspection of this session has been offloaded to the slave unit.
- D. This session cannot be synced with the slave unit.

Correct Answer: B

Question #37

View the IPS exit log, and then answer the question below.

\# diagnose test application ipsmonitor 3

ipsengine exit log"

pid = 93 (cfg), duration = 5605322 (s) at Wed Apr 19 09:57:26 2017
code = 11, reason: manual

What is the status of IPS on this FortiGate?

    A. IPS engine memory consumption has exceeded the model-specific predefined value.

    B. IPS daemon experienced a crash.

    C. There are communication problems between the IPS engine and the management database.

    D. All IPS-related features have been disabled in FortiGate's configuration.

Correct Answer: D

Question #38

View the exhibit, which contains an entry in the session table, and then answer the question below.

```
session info: proto=6 proto_state=11 duration=53 expire=265 timeout=300 flags=00000000
sockflag=00000000
origin-shaper=
reply-shaper=
per_ip_shaper=
ha_id=0 policy_dir=0 tunnel=/ vlan_cos=0/255
user=AALI state=redir log local may_dirty npu nlb none acct-ext
statistic (bytes/packets/allow_err): org=2651/17/1 reply=19130/28/1 tuples=3
tx speed (Bps/kbps): 75/0 rx speed (Bps/kbps): 542/4
orgin->sink: org pre->post, reply pre->post dev=7->6/6->7 gwy=172.20.121.2/10.0.0.2
hook=post dir=org act=snat 192.167.1.100:49545->216.58.216.238:443(172.20.121.96:49545)
hook=pre dir=reply act=dnat 216.58.216.238:443->172.20.121.96:49545 (192.167.1.100:49545)
hook=post dir=reply act=noop 216.58.216.238:443->192.167.1.100:49545 (0.0.0.0:0)
pos/(before, after) 0/(0,0), 0/(0,0)
src_mac=08:5b:0e:6c:7b:7a
misc=0 policy_id=21 auth_info=0 chk_client_info=0 vd=0
serial=007f2948 tos=ff/ff app_list=0 app=0 url_cat=41
dd_type=0 dd_mode=0
npu_state=00000000
npu info: flag=0x00/0x00, offload=0/0, ips_offload=0/0, epid=0/0, ipid=0/0, vlan=0x0000/0x0000
vlifid=0/0, vtag_in=0x0000/0x0000 in_npu=0/0, out_npu=0/0, fwd_en=0/0, qid=0/0
```

Which one of the following statements is true regarding FortiGate's inspection of this session?

- A. FortiGate applied proxy-based inspection.
- B. FortiGate forwarded this session without any inspection.
- C. FortiGate applied flow-based inspection.
- D. FortiGate applied explicit proxy-based inspection.

Correct Answer: A

Question #39

An administrator wants to capture ESP traffic between two FortiGates using the built-in sniffer. If the administrator knows that there is no NAT device located between both FortiGates, what command should the administrator execute?

- A. diagnose sniffer packet any "~udp port 500'
- B. diagnose sniffer packet any "~udp port 4500'

C. diagnose sniffer packet any "~esp'
D. diagnose sniffer packet any "~udp port 500 or udp port 4500'

Correct Answer: C

Question #40

Which of the following conditions must be met for a static route to be active in the routing table? (Choose three.)

    A. The next-hop IP address is up.

    B. There is no other route, to the same destination, with a higher distance.

    C. The link health monitor (if configured) is up.

    D. The next-hop IP address belongs to one of the outgoing interface subnets.

    E. The outgoing interface is up.

Correct Answer: CDE

Question #41

View the exhibit, which contains the partial output of a diagnose command, and then answer the question below.

```
Spoke-2 # dia vpn tunnel list
list all ipsec tunnel in vd 0
name=VPN ver=1 serial=1 10.200.5.1:0->10.200.4.1:0
bound_if=3 lgwy=static/1 tun=intf/0 mode=auto/1 encap=none/0
proxyid_num=1 child_num=0 refcnt=15 ilast=10 olast=792 auto-discovery=0
stat: rxp=0 txp=0 rxb=0 txb=0
dpd: mode=on-demand on=1 idle=20000 ms retry=3 count=0 seqno=0
natt: mode=none draft=0 interval=0 remote_port=0
proxyid=VPN proto=0 sa=1 ref=2 serial=1
  src: 0:10.1.2.0/255.255.0:0
  dst: 0:10.1.1.0/255.255.255.0:0
  SA: ref=3 options=2e type=00 soft=0 mtu=1438 expire=42403/0B replaywin=2048 seqno=1 esn=0
replaywin_lastseq=00000000
  life: type=01 bytes=0/0 timeout=43177/43200
  dec: spi=ccc1f66d esp=aes key=16 280e5cd6f9bacc65ac771556c464ffbd
      ah=sha1 key=20 c68091d69753578785de6a7a6b276b506c527efe
  enc: spi=df14200b esp=aes key=16 b02a7e9f5542b69aff6aa391738ee393
      ah=sha1 key20 889f7529887c215c25950be2ba83e6fe1a5367be
  dec:pkts/bytes=0/0, enc:pkts/bytes=0/0
```

Based on the output, which of the following statements is correct?

A. Anti-reply is enabled.
B. DPD is disabled.
C. Quick mode selectors are disabled.
D. Remote gateway IP is 10.200.5.1.

Correct Answer: A

Question #42

View the exhibit, which contains the partial output of an IKE real-time debug, and then answer the question below.

```
ike 0:c49e59846861b0f6/0000000000000000:278: responder: main mode get 1st message..
ike 0:c49e59846861b0f6/0000000000000000:278: incoming proposal:
ike 0:c49e59846861b0f6/0000000000000000:278: proposal id = 0:
ike 0:c49e59846861b0f6/0000000000000000:278:    protocol id = ISAKMP:
ike 0:c49e59846861b0f6/0000000000000000:278:       trans_id = KEY_IKE.
ike 0:c49e59846861b0f6/0000000000000000:278:       encapsulation = IKE/none
ike 0:c49e59846861b0f6/0000000000000000:278:          type=OAKLEY_ENCRYPT_ALG, val=3DES_CBC.
ike 0:c49e59846861b0f6/0000000000000000:278:          type=OAKLEY_HASH_ALG, val=SHA2_256.
ike 0:c49e59846861b0f6/0000000000000000:278:          type=AUTH_METHOD, val=PRESHARED_KEY.
ike 0:c49e59846861b0f6/0000000000000000:278:          type=OAKLEY_GROUP, val=MODP2048.
ike 0:c49e59846861b0f6/0000000000000000:278: ISAKMP SA lifetime=86400
...
ike 0:c49e59846861b0f6/0000000000000000:278: my proposal, gw VPN:
ike 0:c49e59846861b0f6/0000000000000000:278: proposal id = 1:
ike 0:c49e59846861b0f6/0000000000000000:278:    protocol id = ISAKMP:
ike 0:c49e59846861b0f6/0000000000000000:278:       trans_id = KEY_IKE.
ike 0:c49e59846861b0f6/0000000000000000:278:       encapsulation = IKE/none
ike 0:c49e59846861b0f6/0000000000000000:278:          type=OAKLEY_ENCRYPT_ALG, val=AES_CBC,
key-len=256
ike 0:c49e59846861b0f6/0000000000000000:278:          type=OAKLEY_HASH_ALG, val=SHA2_256.
ike 0:c49e59846861b0f6/0000000000000000:278:          type=AUTH_METHOD, val=PRESHARED_KEY.
ike 0:c49e59846861b0f6/0000000000000000:278:          type=OAKLEY_GROUP, val=MODP2048.
ike 0:c49e59846861b0f6/0000000000000000:278: ISAKMP SA lifetime=86400
...
ike 0:c49e59846861b0f6/0000000000000000:278: negotiation failure
ike Negotiate ISAKMP SA Error: ike 0:c49e59846861b0f6/0000000000000000:278:
proposal chosen
...
```

Why didn't the tunnel come up?

    A.   The pre-shared keys do not match.

    B.   The remote gateway's phase 2 configuration does not match the local gateway's phase 2 configuration.

    C.   The remote gateway's phase 1 configuration does not match the local gateway's phase 1 configuration.

    D.   The remote gateway is using aggressive mode and the local gateway is configured to use man mode.

Correct Answer: C

Question #43

An administrator has configured two FortiGate devices for an HA cluster. While testing the HA failover, the administrator noticed that some of the switches in the network continue to send traffic to the former primary unit. The administrator decides to enable the setting link-failed-signal to fix the problem. Which statement is correct regarding this command?

A. Forces the former primary device to shut down all its non-heartbeat interfaces for one second while the failover occurs.

B. Sends an ARP packet to all connected devices, indicating that the HA virtual MAC address is reachable through a new master after a failover.

C. Sends a link failed signal to all connected devices.

D. Disables all the non-heartbeat interfaces in all the HA members for two seconds after a failover.

Correct Answer: A

Question #44

View these partial outputs from two routing debug commands:

```
# get router info kernel
tab=254 vf=0 scope=0 type=1 proto=11 prio=0 0.0.0.0/0.0.0.0/0->0.0.0.0/0 pref=0.0.0.0 gwy=10.200.1.254
dev=2(port1)
tab=254 vf=0 scope=0 type=1 proto=11 prio=0 0.0.0.0/0.0.0.0/0->0.0.0.0/0 pref=0.0.0.0 gwy=10.200.2.254
dev=3(port2)
tab=254 vf=0 scope=253 type=1 proto=2 prio=0 0.0.0.0/0.0.0.0/0->10.0.1.0/24 pref=10.0.1.254 gwy=0.0.0.0
dev=4(port3)
# get router info routing-table all
S*       0.0.0.0/0 [10/0] via 10.200.1.254, port1
                   [10/0] via 10.200.2.254, port2, [10/0]
C        10.0.1.0/24 is directly connected, port3
C        10.200.1.0/24 is directly connected, port1
C        10.200.2.0/24 is directly connected, port2
```

Which outbound interface will FortiGate use to route web traffic from internal users to the Internet?

A. Both port1 and port2

B. port3

35

C. port1

D. port2

Correct Answer: A

Question #45

What conditions are required for two FortiGate devices to form an OSPF adjacency? (Choose three.)

    A. IP addresses are in the same subnet.

    B. Hello and dead intervals match.

    C. OSPF IP MTUs match.

    D. OSPF peer IDs match.

    E. OSPF costs match.

Correct Answer: ABC

Question #46

View the exhibit, which contains the output of a debug command, and then answer the question below.

```
# get router info ospf interface port4
port4 is up, line protocol is up
    Internet Address 172.20.121.236/24, Area 0.0.0.0, MTU 1500
    Process ID 0, Router ID 0.0.0.4, Network Type BROADCAST, Cost: 1
    Transmit Delay is 1 sec, State DROther, Priority 1
    Designated Router (ID) 172.20.140.2, Interface Address 172.20.121.2
Backup Designated Router (ID) 0.0.0.1, Interface Address 172.20.121.239
Timer intervals configured, Hello 10.000, Dead 40, Wait 40, Retransmit 5
        Hello due in 00:00:05
    Neighbor Count is 4, Adjacent neighbor count is 2
    Crypt Sequence Number is 411
    Hello received 106, sent 27, DD received 7 sent 9
    LS-Req received 2 sent 2, LS-Upd received 7 sent 5
    LS-Ack received 4 sent 3, Discarded 1
```

Which of the following statements about the exhibit are true? (Choose two.)

A.   In the network on port4, two OSPF routers are down.

B.   Port4 is connected to the OSPF backbone area.

C.   The local FortiGate's OSPF router ID is 0.0.0.4

D.   The local FortiGate has been elected as the OSPF backup designated router.

Correct Answer: BC

Question #47

How does FortiManager handle FortiGuard requests from FortiGate devices, when it is configured as a local FDS?

A.   FortiManager can download and maintain local copies of FortiGuard databases.

B.   FortiManager supports only FortiGuard push to managed devices.

C. FortiManager will respond to update requests only if they originate from a managed device.

D. FortiManager does not support rating requests.

Correct Answer: A

Question #48

View the exhibit, which contains the output of a real-time debug, and then answer the question below.

```
# diagnose debug application urlfilter -1
# diagnose debug enable

msg="received a request /tmp/.ipsengine_498_0_0.url.socket, addr_len=37:
d=www.fortinet.com:80
id=83, vfname='root', vfid=0, profile='default', type=0, client=10.0.1.10,
url_source=1, url="/"
msg="Found it in cache.   URL cat=52" IP cat=52user="N/A" src=10.0.1.10
sport=60348 dst=66.171.121.44 dport=80 service="http" hostname="
www.fortinet.com" url="/" matchType=prefix
action=10(ftgd-block) wf-act=3(BLOCK) user="N/A" src=10.0.1.10 sport=60348
dst=66.171.121.44
dport=80 service="http" cat=52 cat desc="Information Technology"
hostname="fortinet.com"
url="/"
```

Which of the following statements is true regarding this output? (Choose two.)

A. This web request was inspected using the root web filter profile.

B. FortiGate found the requested URL in its local cache.

C. The requested URL belongs to category ID 52.

D. The web request was allowed by FortiGate.

Correct Answer: BC

Question #49

What is the purpose of an internal segmentation firewall (ISFW)?

- A. It inspects incoming traffic to protect services in the corporate DMZ.
- B. It is the first line of defense at the network perimeter.
- C. It splits the network into multiple security segments to minimize the impact of breaches.
- D. It is an all-in-one security appliance that is placed at remote sites to extend the enterprise network.

Correct Answer: C

Question #50

View the exhibit, which contains the partial output of an IKE real-time debug, and then answer the question below. ike 0: comes 10.0.0.2:500->10.0.0.1:500, ifindex=7.... ike 0: IKEv1 exchange=Aggressive id=baf47d0988e9237f/2f405ef3952f6fda len=430 ike 0: in BAF47D0988E9237F2F405EF3952F6FDA011004000000000000000001 AE0400003C0000000100000001000000300101000 ike 0:RemoteSite:4: initiator: aggressive mode get 1st response... ike 0:RemoteSite:4: VID RFC 3947 4A131c81070358455C5728F20E95452F ike 0:RemoteSite:4:

VID   DPD   AFCAD71368A1F1C96B8696FC77570100   ike
0:RemoteSite:4:   VID   FORTIGATE
8299031757A36082C6A621DE000502D7 ike 0:RemoteSite:4: peer is
FortiGate/Fortios   (v5   b727)   ike   0:RemoteSite:4:   VID
FRAGMENTATION   4048B7D56EBCE88525E7DE7F00D6C2D3
ike   0:RemoteSite:4:   VID   FRAGMENTATION
4048B7D56EBCE88525E7DE7F00D6C2D3C0000000   ike
0:RemoteSite:4: received peer identifier FQDN "~remore' ike
0:RemoteSite:4: negotiation result ike 0:RemoteSite:4: proposal id = 1:
ike 0:RemoteSite:4: protocol id = ISAKMP: ike 0:RemoteSite:4:
trans_id = KEY_IKE. ike 0:RemoteSite:4: encapsulation = IKE/none
ike   0:RemoteSite:4:   type=OAKLEY_ENCRYPT_ALG,
val=AES_CBC,   key   ""len=128   ike   0:RemoteSite:4:
type=OAKLEY_HASH_ALG, val=SHA. ike 0:RemoteSite:4: type-
AUTH_METHOD, val=PRESHARED_KEY. ike 0:RemoteSite:4:
type=OAKLEY_GROUP, val=MODP1024. ike 0:RemoteSite:4:
ISAKMP SA lifetime=86400 ike 0:RemoteSite:4: ISAKMP SA
baf47d0988e9237f/2f405ef3952f6fda   key   16:
B25B6C9384D8BDB24E3DA3DC90CF5E73 ike 0:RemoteSite:4: PSK
authentication succeeded ike 0:RemoteSite:4: authentication OK ike
0:RemoteSite:4: add INITIAL-CONTACT ike 0:RemoteSite:4: enc
BAF47D0988E9237F405EF3952F6FDA0810040100000000000000801
40000181F2E48BFD8E9D603F   ike   0:RemoteSite:4:   out
BAF47D0988E9237F405EF3952F6FDA0810040100000000000000008C
2E3FC9BA061816A396F009A12 ike 0:RemoteSite:4: sent IKE msg
(agg_i2send):   10.0.0.1:500-10.0.0.2:500,   len=140,
id=baf47d0988e9237f/2 ike 0:RemoteSite:4: established IKE SA
baf47d0988e9237f/2f405ef3952f6fda

Which statements about this debug output are correct? (Choose two.)

    A.   The remote gateway IP address is 10.0.0.1.
    B.   It shows a phase 1 negotiation.
    C.   The negotiation is using AES128 encryption with CBC hash.
    D.   The initiator has provided remote as its IPsec peer ID.

Correct Answer: BD

Question #51

Which of the following statements are correct regarding application layer test commands? (Choose two.)

- A. They are used to filter real-time debugs.
- B. They display real-time application debugs.
- C. Some of them display statistics and configuration information about a feature or process.
- D. Some of them can be used to restart an application.

Correct Answer: CD

Question #52

When using the SSL certificate inspection method for HTTPS traffic, how does FortiGate filter web requests when the browser client does not provide the server name indication (SNI)?

- A. FortiGate uses the Issued To: field in the server's certificate.
- B. FortiGate switches to the full SSL inspection method to decrypt the data.
- C. FortiGate blocks the request without any further inspection.

D. FortiGate uses the requested URL from the user's web browser.

Correct Answer: A

Question #53

What global configuration setting changes the behavior for content-inspected traffic while FortiGate is in system conserve mode?

    A.   av-failopen
    B.   mem-failopen
    C.   utm-failopen
    D.   ips-failopen

Correct Answer: A

Question #54

View the exhibit, which contains the output of a BGP debug command, and then answer the question below.

```
# get router info bgp summary
BGP router identifier 0.0.0.117, local AS number 65117
BGP table version is 104
3 BGP AS-PATH entries
0 BGP community entries

Neighbor      V    AS   MsgRcvd  MsgSent  TblVer  InQ  OutQ  Up/Down    State/PfxRcd
10.125.0.60   4  65060  1698       1756     103     0     0  03:02:49        1
10.127.0.75   4  65075  2206       2250     102     0     0  02:45:55        1
10.200.3.1    4  65501  101         115       0     0     0  never       Active

Total number of neighbors 3
```

Which of the following statements about the exhibit are true? (Choose two.)

A. For the peer 10.125.0.60, the BGP state of is Established.
B. The local BGP peer has received a total of three BGP prefixes.
C. Since the BGP counters were last reset, the BGP peer 10.200.3.1 has never been down.
D. The local BGP peer has not established a TCP session to the BGP peer 10.200.3.1.

Correct Answer: AD

Question #55

View the exhibit, which contains the output of a web diagnose command, and then answer the question below.

diagnose webfilter fortiguard statistics list

Raring Statistics:
====================================

DNS filures	:	273
DNS lookups	:	280
Data send failures	:	0
Data read failures	:	0
Wrong package type	:	0
Hash table miss	:	0
Unknown server	:	0
Incorrect CRC	:	0
Proxy requests failures	:	0
Request timeout	:	1
Total requests	:	2409
Requests to FortiGuard servers	:	1182
Server errored responses	:	0
Relayed rating	:	0
Invalid profile	:	0
Allowed	:	1021
Blocked	:	3909
Logged	:	3927
Blocked Errors	:	565
Allowed Errors	:	0
Monitors	:	0
Authenticates	:	0
Warnings	:	18
Ovrd request timeout	:	0
Ovrd send failures	:	0
Ovrd read failures	:	0
Ovrd errored responses	:	0
...		

diagnose webfilter fortiguard statistics list

Cache Statistics:
====================================

Maximum memory	:	0
Memory usage	:	0
Nodes	:	0
Leaves	:	0
Prefix nodes	:	0
Exact nodes	:	0
Requests	:	0
Misses	:	0
Hits	:	0
Prefix hits	:	0
Exact hits	:	0
No cache directives	:	0
Add after prefix	:	0
Invalid DB put	:	0
DB updates	:	0
Percent full	:	0%
Branches	:	0%
Leaves	:	0%
Prefix nodes	:	0%
Exact nodes	:	0%
Miss rate	:	0%
Hit rate	:	0%
Prefix hits	:	0%
Exact hits	:	0%

Which one of the following statements explains why the cache statistics are all zeros?

A. The administrator has reallocated the cache memory to a separate process.

B. There are no users making web requests.

C. The FortiGuard web filter cache is disabled in the FortiGate's configuration.

D. FortiGate is using a flow-based web filter and the cache applies only to proxy-based inspection.

Correct Answer: C

Question #56

View the exhibit, which contains a partial output of an IKE real-time debug, and then answer the question below.

```
ike 0:H2S_0_1: shortcut 10.200.5.1.:0  10.1.2.254->10.1.1.254

...
ike 0:H2S_0_1:15: sent IKE msg (SHORTCUT-OFFER): 10.200.1.1:500->10.200.5.1:500,
len=164, id=4134df8580d5cdd/ce54851612c7432f:a21f14fe
ike 0: comes 10.200.5.1:500->10.200.1.1:500,ifindex=3....
ike 0: IKEv1 exchange=Informational id=4134df8580d5bcdd/ce54851612c7432f:6266ee8c
len=196

ike 0:H2S_0_1:15: notify msg received: SHORTCUR-QUERY
ike 0:H2S_0_1: recv shortcut-query 16462343159772385317

ike 0:H2S_0_0:16: senr IKE msg (SHORTCUT-QUERY): 10.200.1.1:500->10.200.3.1:500,
len=196, id=7c6b6cca6700a935/dba061eaf51b89f7:b326df2a
ike 0: comes 10.200.3.1:500->10.200.1.1:500,ifindex=3....
ike 0: IKEv1 exchange=Informational id=7c6b6cca6700a935/dba061eaf51b89f7:1c1dbf39
len=188

ike 0:H2S_0_0:16: notify msg received: SHORTCUT-REPLY
ike 0:H2S_0_0: recv shortcut-reply 16462343159772385317
f97a7565a441e2aa/667d3e2e3442211e 10.200.3.1 to 10.1.2.254 psk 64
ike 0:H2S_0_0: shortcut-reply route to 10.1.2.254 via H2S_0_1 29
ike 0:H2S: forward shortcut-reply 16462343159772385317
f97a7565a441e2aa/667d3e2e3442211e 10.200.3.1 to 10.1.2.254 psk 64 ttl 31
ike 0:H2S_0_1:15: enc
...
ike 0:H2S_0_1:15: sent IKE msg (SHORTCUT-REPLY): 10.200.1.1:500->10.200.5.1:500,
len=188, id=4134df8580d5bcdd/ce54851612c7432f:70ed6d2c
```

Based on the debug output, which phase-1 setting is enabled in the configuration of this VPN?

- A.   auto-discovery-sender
- B.   auto-discovery-forwarder
- C.   auto-discovery-shortcut
- D.   auto-discovery-receiver

Correct Answer: A

Question #57

View the global IPS configuration, and then answer the question below.

```
config ips global
    set fail-open disable
    set intelligent-mode disable
    set engine-count 0
    set algorithm engine-pick
end
```

Which of the following statements is true regarding this configuration?

A. IPS will scan every byte in every session.
B. FortiGate will spawn IPS engine instances based on the system load.
C. New packets will be passed through without inspection if the IPS socket buffer runs out of memory.
D. IPS will use the faster matching algorithm which is only available for units with more than 4 GB memory.

Correct Answer: A

Question #58

View the following FortiGate configuration.

```
config system global
    set snat-route-change disable
end
config router static
    edit 1
        set gateway 10.200.1.254
        set priority 5
        set device "port1"
    next
    edit 2
        set gateway 10.200.2.254
        set priority 10
        set device "port2"
    next
end
```

All traffic to the Internet currently egresses from port1. The exhibit shows partial session information for Internet traffic from a user on the internal network:

```
# diagnose sys session list
session info: proto=6 proto_state+01 duration=17 expire=7 timeout=3600
flags=00000000 sockflag=00000000 sockport=0 av_idx=0 use=3
ha_id=0 policy_dir=0 tunnel=/
state=may_dirty none app_ntf
statistic(bytes/packets/allow_err): org=57555/7/1 reply=23367/19/1 tuples=2
orgin->sink: org pre->post, reply pre->post dev=4->2/2->4
gwy=10.200.1.254/10.0.1.10
hook=post dir=org act=snat 10.0.1.10:64907-
>54.239.158.170:80(10.200.1.1:64907)
hook=pre dir=reply act=dnat 54.239.158.170:80-
>10.200.1.1:64907(10.0.1.10:64907)
pos/(before, after) 0/(0,0), 0/(0,0)
misc=0 policy_id=1 auth_info=0 chk_client_info=0 vd=0
serial=00000294 tos=ff/ff ips_view=0 app_list=0 app=0
dd_type=0 dd_mode=0
```

If the priority on route ID 1 were changed from 5 to 20, what would happen to traffic matching that user's session?

    A. The session would remain in the session table, and its traffic would still egress from port1.

    B. The session would remain in the session table, but its traffic would now egress from both port1 and port2.

    C. The session would remain in the session table, and its traffic would start to egress from port2.

    D. The session would be deleted, so the client would need to start a new session.

Correct Answer: A

Question #59

View the exhibit, which contains the output of a diagnose command, and then answer the question below.

```
# diagnose debug rating
Locale        : english
License       : Contract
Expiration    : Thu Sep 28 17:00:00 20xx
-=- Server List (Thu Apr 19 10:41:32 20xx) -=-
```

IP	Weight	RTT	Flags	TZ	Packets	Curr Lost	Total Lost
64.26.151.37	10	45		-5	262432	0	846
64.26.151.35	10	46		-5	329072	0	6806
66.117.56.37	10	75		-5	71638	0	275
65.210.95.240	20	71		-8	36875	0	92
209.222.147.36	20	103	DI	-8	34784	0	1070
208.91.112.194	20	107	D	-8	35170	0	1533
96.45.33.65	60	144		0	33728	0	120
80.85.69.41	71	226		1	33797	0	192
62.209.40.74	150	97		9	33754	0	145
121.111.236.179	45	44	F	-5	26410	26226	26227

Which statements are true regarding the output in the exhibit? (Choose two.)

 A. FortiGate will probe 121.111.236.179 every fifteen minutes for a response.

 B. Servers with the D flag are considered to be down.

 C. Servers with a negative TZ value are experiencing a service outage.

 D. FortiGate used 209.222.147.3 as the initial server to validate its contract.

Correct Answer: AD

Question #60

What does the dirty flag mean in a FortiGate session?

- A. Traffic has been blocked by the antivirus inspection.
- B. The next packet must be re-evaluated against the firewall policies.
- C. The session must be removed from the former primary unit after an HA failover.
- D. Traffic has been identified as from an application that is not allowed.

Correct Answer: B

Question #61

The CLI command set intelligent-mode <enable | disable> controls the IPS engine's adaptive scanning behavior. Which of the following statements describes IPS adaptive scanning?

- A. Determines the optimal number of IPS engines required based on system load.
- B. Downloads signatures on demand from FDS based on scanning requirements.
- C. Determines when it is secure enough to stop scanning session traffic.
- D. Choose a matching algorithm based on available memory and the type of inspection being performed.

Correct Answer: C

Question #62

An administrator has configured the following CLI script on FortiManager, which failed to apply any changes to the managed device after being executed.

```
# conf rout stat
#     edit 0
#             set gateway 10.20.121.2
#             set priority 20
#             set device "wan1"
#     next
# end
```

Why didn't the script make any changes to the managed device?

    A. Commands that start with the # sign are not executed.
    B. CLI scripts will add objects only if they are referenced by policies.
    C. Incomplete commands are ignored in CLI scripts.
    D. Static routes can only be added using TCL scripts.

Correct Answer: A

Question #63

View the exhibit, which contains a partial web filter profile configuration, and then answer the question below.

Which action will FortiGate take if a user attempts to access www.dropbox.com, which is categorized as File Sharing and Storage?

    A.   FortiGate will exempt the connection based on the Web Content Filter configuration.

    B.   FortiGate will block the connection based on the URL Filter configuration.

C. FortiGate will allow the connection based on the FortiGuard category based filter configuration.

D. FortiGate will block the connection as an invalid URL.

Correct Answer: B

Question #64

Which configuration can be used to reduce the number of BGP sessions in an IBGP network?

    A. Neighbor range

    B. Route reflector

    C. Next-hop-self

    D. Neighbor group

Correct Answer: B

Question #65

View the exhibit, which contains the output of get sys ha status, and then answer the question below.

```
NGFW # get sys ha status
HA Health Status: ok
Model: FortiGate0VM64
Mode: HA A-P
Group: 0
Debug: 0
Cluster Uptime: 0 days 01:07:35
Master selected using:
  <2017/04/24 09:43:44> FGVM010000077649 is selected as the master because it has the largest value of override pr
  <2017/04/24 08:50:53> FGVM010000077 is selected as the master because it's the only member in the cluster.
ses_pickup: disable
override: enable
Configuration Status:
  FGVM010000077649(updated 1 seconds ago): in-sync
  FGVM010000077650(updated 0 seconds ago): out-of-sync
System Usage stats:
  FGVM010000077649(updated 1 seconds ago):
    sessions=30, average-cpu-user/nice/system/idle=0%/0%/0%/100%, memory-60%
  FGVM010000077650(updated 0 seconds ago):
    sessions=2, average-cpu-user/nice/system/idle=0%/0%/0%/100%, memory-61%
HBDEV stats:
  FGVM010000077649(updated 1 seconds ago):
    port7: physical/10000full, up, rx-bytes/packets/dropped/errors=7358367/17029/25/0, tx=7721830/17182/0/0
  FGVM010000077650(updated 0 seconds ago):
    port7: physical/10000full, up, rx-bytes/packets/dropped/errors=7793722/17190/0/0, tx=8940374/20806/0/0
Master: NGFW      , FGVM010000077649
Slave : NGFW-2    , FGVM010000077650
number of vcluster: 1
vcluster 1: work 169.254.0.2
Master:0 FGVM0100000077649
Slave :1 FGVM0100000077650
```

Which statements are correct regarding the output? (Choose two.)

    A.   The slave configuration is not synchronized with the master.

    B.   The HA management IP is 169.254.0.2.

    C.   Master is selected because it is the only device in the cluster.

    D.   port 7 is used the HA heartbeat on all devices in the cluster.

Correct Answer: AD

Question #66

View the exhibit, which contains the partial output of an IKE real time debug, and then answer the question below.

```
ike 0:9268ab9dea63aa3/0000000000000000:591: responder: main mode get 1st message..
ike 0:9268ab9dea63aa3/0000000000000000:591: incoming proposal:
ike 0:9268ab9dea63aa3/0000000000000000:591: proposal id = 0:
ike 0:9268ab9dea63aa3/0000000000000000:591:     protocol id = ISAKMP:
ike 0:9268ab9dea63aa3/0000000000000000:591:        trans_id = KEY_IKE.
ike 0:9268ab9dea63aa3/0000000000000000:591:        encapsulation = IKE/none
ike 0:9268ab9dea63aa3/0000000000000000:591:           type=OAKLEY_ENCRYPT_ALG, val=3DES_CBC.
ike 0:9268ab9dea63aa3/0000000000000000:591:           type=OAKLEY_HASH_ALG, val=SHA2_256.
ike 0:9268ab9dea63aa3/0000000000000000:591:           type=AUTH_METHOD, val=PRESHARED_KEY.
ike 0:9268ab9dea63aa3/0000000000000000:591:           type=OAKLEY_GROUP, val=MODP1536.
ike 0:9268ab9dea63aa3/0000000000000000:591: ISAKMP SA lifetime=86400
ike 0:9268ab9dea63aa3/0000000000000000:591: proposal id=0:
ike 0:9268ab9dea63aa3/0000000000000000:591:     protocol id = ISAKMP:
ike 0:9268ab9dea63aa3/0000000000000000:591:        trans_id = KEY_IKE.
ike 0:9268ab9dea63aa3/0000000000000000:591:        encapsulation = IKE/none
ike 0:9268ab9dea63aa3/0000000000000000:591:           type=OAKLEY_ENCRYPT_ALG, val=3DES_CBC.
ike 0:9268ab9dea63aa3/0000000000000000:591:           type=OAKLEY_HASH_ALG, val=SHA2_256.
ike 0:9268ab9dea63aa3/0000000000000000:591:           type=AUTH_METHOD, val=PRESHARED_KEY.
ike 0:9268ab9dea63aa3/0000000000000000:591:           type=OAKLEY_GROUP, val=MODP1536.
ike 0:9268ab9dea63aa3/0000000000000000:591: ISA KMP SA lifetime=86400
ike 0:9268ab9dea63aa3/0000000000000000:591: my proposal, gw VPN:
ike 0:9268ab9dea63aa3/0000000000000000:591:     proposal id = 1:
ike 0:9268ab9dea63aa3/0000000000000000:591:        protocol id = ISAKMP:
ike 0:9268ab9dea63aa3/0000000000000000:591:           trans_id = KEY_IKE.
ike 0:9268ab9dea63aa3/0000000000000000:591:           encapsulation = IKE/none
ike 0:9268ab9dea63aa3/0000000000000000:591:              type=OAKLEY_ENCRYPT_ALG, val=AES_CBC,
key-len=128
ike 0:9268ab9dea63aa3/0000000000000000:591:              type=OAKLEY_HASH_ALG, val=SHA2_512.
ike 0:9268ab9dea63aa3/0000000000000000:591:              type=AUTH_METHOD, val=PRESHARED_KEY.
ike 0:9268ab9dea63aa3/0000000000000000:591:              type=OAKLEY_GROUP, val=MODP2048.
ike 0:9268ab9dea63aa3/0000000000000000:591: ISAKMP SA lifetime=86400
ike 0:9268ab9dea63aa3/0000000000000000:591: proposal id = 1:
ike 0:9268ab9dea63aa3/0000000000000000:591:        protocol id = ISAKMP:
ike 0:9268ab9dea63aa3/0000000000000000:591:        trans_id = KEY_IKE.
ike 0:9268ab9dea63aa3/0000000000000000:591:        encapsulation = IKE/none
ike 0:9268ab9dea63aa3/0000000000000000:591:              type=OAKLEY_ENCRYPT_ALG, val=AES_CBC,
key-len=128
ike 0:9268ab9dea63aa3/0000000000000000:591:              type=OAKLEY_HASH_ALG, val=SHA2_512.
ike 0:9268ab9dea63aa3/0000000000000000:591:              type=AUTH_METHOD, val=PRESHARED_KEY.
ike 0:9268ab9dea63aa3/0000000000000000:591:              type=OAKLEY_GROUP, val=MODP2048.
ike 0:9268ab9dea63aa3/0000000000000000:591: ISAKMP SA lifetime=86400
ike 0:9268ab9dea63aa3/0000000000000000:591: proposal id = 1:
ike 0:9268ab9dea63aa3/0000000000000000:591:        protocol id = ISAKMP:
ike 0:9268ab9dea63aa3/0000000000000000:591:        trans_id = ISAKMP:
ike 0:9268ab9dea63aa3/0000000000000000:591:        encapsulation = IKE/none
ike 0:9268ab9dea63aa3/0000000000000000:591:              type=OAKLEY_ENCRYPT_ALG, val =AES-CBC,
key-len=128
ike 0:9268ab9dea63aa3/0000000000000000:591:              type=OAKLEY_HASH_ALG, val=SHA2_512.
ike 0:9268ab9dea63aa3/0000000000000000:591:              type=AUTH_METHOD, val=PRESHARED_KEY.
ike 0:9268ab9dea63aa3/0000000000000000:591:              type=OAKLEY_GROUP, val=MODP1536.
ike 0:9268ab9dea63aa3/0000000000000000:591: ISAKMP SA lifetime=86400
```

The administrator does not have access to the remote gateway. Based on the debug output, what configuration changes can the administrator make to the local gateway to resolve the phase 1 negotiation error?

- A. Change phase 1 encryption to AESCBC and authentication to SHA128.
- B. Change phase 1 encryption to 3DES and authentication to CBC.
- C. Change phase 1 encryption to AES128 and authentication to SHA512.
- D. Change phase 1 encryption to 3DES and authentication to SHA256.

Correct Answer: C

Question #67

View the exhibit, which contains the output of a diagnose command, and the answer the question below.

```
# diagnose debug rating
Locale       : English
License      : Contract
Expiration   : Thu Sep 28 17:00:00 20XX
-=- Server List (Thu APR 19 10:41:32 20XX) -=-
IP                Weight   RTT   Flags   TZ   Packets   Curr Lost   Total Lost
64.26.151.37      10       45            -5   262432    0           846
64.26.151.35      10       46            -5   329072    0           6806
66.117.56.37      10       75            -5   71638     0           275
66.210.95.240     20       71            -8   36875     0           92
209.222.147.36    20       103   DI      -8   34784     0           1070
208.91.112.194    20       107   D       -8   35170     0           1533
96.45.33.65       60       144           0    33728     0           120
80.85.69.41       71       226           1    33797     0           192
62.209.40.74      150      97            9    33754     0           145
121.111.236.179   45       44    F       -5   26410     26226       26227
```

Which statements are true regarding the Weight value?

    A.   Its initial value is calculated based on the round trip delay (RTT).

    B.   Its initial value is statically set to 10.

    C.   Its value is incremented with each packet lost.

    D.   It determines which FortiGuard server is used for license validation.

Correct Answer: C

Question #68

In which of the following states is a given session categorized as ephemeral? (Choose two.)

    A. A TCP session waiting to complete the three-way handshake.

    B. A TCP session waiting for FIN ACK.

    C. A UDP session with packets sent and received.

    D. A UDP session with only one packet received.

Correct Answer: AD

Question #69

View the exhibit, which contains a session entry, and then answer the question below.

```
session info: proto=1 proto_state=00 duration=1 expire=59 timeout=0 flags=00000000
sockflag=00000000 sockport=0 av_idx=0 use=3
origin-shaper=
reply-shaper=
per_ip_shaper=
ha_id=0 policy_dir=0 tunnel=/ vlan_cos=0/255
state=log may_dirty none
statistic(bytes/packets/allow_err): org=168/2/1 reply=168/2/1 tuples=2
tx speed(Bps/kbps): 97/0 rx speed(Bps/kbps): 97/0
orgin->sink: org pre->post, reply pre->post dev=9->3/3->9 gwy=10.200.1.254/10.1.0.1
hook=post dir=org act=snat 10.1.10.10:40602->10.200.5.1:8(10.200.1.254/10.1.0.1
hook=pre dir=reply act=dnat 10.200.5.1:60430->10.200.1.1:0(10.1.10.10:40602)
misc=0 policy_id=1 auth_info=0 chk_client_info=0 vd=0
serial=0002a5c9 tos=ff/ff app_list=0 app=0 url_cat=0
dd_type=0 dd_mode=0
```

Which statement is correct regarding this session?

    A. It is an ICMP session from 10.1.10.10 to 10.200.1.1.

    B. It is an ICMP session from 10.1.10.10 to 10.200.5.1.

C. It is a TCP session in ESTABLISHED state from 10.1.10.10 to 10.200.5.1.

D. It is a TCP session in CLOSE_WAIT state from 10.1.10.10 to 10.200.1.1.

Correct Answer: B

Question #70

View the exhibit, which contains a screenshot of some phase-1 settings, and then answer the question below.

The VPN is up, and DPD packets are being exchanged between both IPsec gateways; however, traffic cannot pass through the tunnel. To diagnose, the administrator enters these CLI commands:

However, the IKE real time debug does not show any output. Why?

A. The debug output shows phases 1 and 2 negotiations only. Once the tunnel is up, it does not show any more output.

B. The log-filter setting was set incorrectly. The VPN's traffic does not match this filter.

C. The debug shows only error messages. If there is no output, then the tunnel is operating normally.

D. The debug output shows phase 1 negotiation only. After that, the administrator must enable the following real time debug: diagnose debug application ipsec -1.

Correct Answer: B

Question #71

View the exhibit, which contains the output of a diagnose command, and then answer the question below.

```
     diagnose sys session list expectation

session info: proto=6 proto_state-00 duration=3 expire=26 timeout=3600 flags=00000000
sockflag=00000000 sockport=0 av_idx=0 use=3
origin-shaper=
reply-shaper=
ha_id-0 policy_dir=1 tunnel=/
state=new complex
statistic(bytes/packets/allow_err): org-0/0/0 reply-0/0/0 tuples=2
orgin->sink: org pre->post, reply pre->post dev=2->4/4->2 gwy=10.0.1.10/10.200.1.254
hook=pre dir-org act=dnat 10.171.121.38:0->10.200.1.1:60426(10.0.1.10:50365)
hook=pre dir-org act=noop 0.0.0.0:0->0.0.0.0:0(0.0.0.0:0)
pos/(before, after) 0/(0,0), 0/(0,0)
misc=0 policy_id=1 auth_info=0 chk_client_info=0 vd=0
serial=000000e9 tos=ff/ff ips_view=0 app_list=0 app=0
dd_type=0 dd_mode=0
```

What statements are correct regarding the output? (Choose two.)

A. This is an expected session created by a session helper.

B. Traffic in the original direction (coming from the IP address 10.171.122.38) will be routed to the next-hop IP address 10.0.1.10.

C. Traffic in the original direction (coming from the IP address 10.171.122.38) will be routed to the next-hop IP address 10.200.1.1.

D. This is an expected session created by an application control profile.

Correct Answer: AC

Question #72

Which of the following statements are true about FortiManager when it is deployed as a local FDS? (Choose two.)

A. Caches available firmware updates for unmanaged devices.
B. Can be configured as an update server, or a rating server, but not both.
C. Supports rating requests from both managed and unmanaged devices.
D. Provides VM license validation services.

Correct Answer: CD

Question #73

Which statement is true regarding File description (FD) conserve mode?

A. IPS inspection is affected when FortiGate enters FD conserve mode.
B. A FortiGate enters FD conserve mode when the amount of available description is less than 5%.
C. FD conserve mode affects all daemons running on the device.
D. Restarting the WAD process is required to leave FD conserve mode.

Correct Answer: B

- More Questions.

Question #74

A FortiGate device has the following LDAP configuration:

```
config user ldap
    edit "WindowsLDAP"
        set server "10.0.1.10"
        set cnid "cn"
        set dn "cn=Users, dc=trainingAD, dc=training, dc=lab"
        set type regular
        set username "dc=trainingAD, dc=training, dc=lab"
        set password xxxxxxx
    next
end
```

The administrator executed the 'dsquery' command in the Windows LDAP server 10.0.1.10, and got the following output:

>dsquery user -samid administrator

"CN=Administrator, CN=Users, DC=trainingAD, DC=training, DC=lab"

Based on the output, what FortiGate LDAP setting is configured incorrectly?

A. cnid.
B. username.
C. password.
D. dn.

Correct Answer: B

Question #75

Examine the following partial output from two system debug commands; then answer the question below.

diagnose hardware sysinfo memory

MemTotal: 3092728 kB

MemFree: 1954204 kB

MemShared: 0 kB

Buffers: 284 kB

Cached: 143004 kB

SwapCached: 0 kB

Active: 34092 kB

Inactive: 109256 kB

HighTotal 1179648 kB

HighFree: 853516 kB

LowTotal: 1913080 kB

LowFree: 1100688 kB

SwapTotal: 0 kB

SwapFree: 0 kB

diagnose hardware sysinfo shm

SHM counter: 285

SHM allocated: 6823936

SHM total: 623452160

concervemode: 0

shm last entered: n/a

system last entered: n/a

SHM FS total: 639725568

SHM FS free: 632614912

SHM FS avail: 632614912

SHM FS alloc: 7110656

Which of the following statements are true regarding the above outputs? (Choose two.)

- A. The unit is running a 32-bit FortiOS
- B. The unit is in kernel conserve mode
- C. The Cached value is always the Active value plus the Inactive value
- D. Kernel indirectly accesses the low memory (LowTotal) through memory paging

Correct Answer: AC

Question #76

Examine the following partial output from a sniffer command; then answer the question below.

diagnose sniff packet any icmp 4

interfaces=[any]

filters=[icmp]

2.101199 wan2 in 192.168.1.110 -> 4.2.2.2: icmp: echo request

2.1011400 wan1 out 172.17.87.16 -> 4.2.2.2: icmp: echo request

.....

2.123500 wan2 out 4.2.2.2 -> 192.168.1.110: icmp: echo reply

244 packets received by filter

5 packets dropped by kernel

What is the meaning of the packets dropped counter at the end of the sniffer?

- A. Number of packets that didn't match the sniffer filter.
- B. Number of total packets dropped by the FortiGate.
- C. Number of packets that matched the sniffer filter and were dropped by the FortiGate.
- D. Number of packets that matched the sniffer filter but could not be captured by the sniffer.

Correct Answer: D

Question #77

Examine the output from the 'diagnose debug authd fsso list' command; then answer the question below.

diagnose debug authd fsso list

----FSSO logons----

IP: 192.168.3.1 User: STUDENT Groups: TRAININGAD/USERS Workstation: INTERNAL2. TRAINING. LAB

The IP address 192.168.3.1 is NOT the one used by the workstation INTERNAL2. TRAINING. LAB.

What should the administrator check?

- A. The IP address recorded in the logon event for the user STUDENT.
- B. The DNS name resolution for the workstation name INTERNAL2. TRAINING. LAB.
- C. The source IP address of the traffic arriving to the FortiGate from the workstation INTERNAL2. TRAINING. LAB.
- D. The reserve DNS lookup for the IP address 192.168.3.1.

Correct Answer: B

Question #78

A FortiGate's port1 is connected to a private network. Its port2 is connected to the Internet. Explicit web proxy is enabled in port1 and only explicit web proxy users can access the Internet. Web cache is

NOT enabled. An internal web proxy user is downloading a file from the Internet via HTTP. Which statements are true regarding the two entries in the FortiGate session table related with this traffic? (Choose two.)

- A. Both session have the local flag on.
- B. The destination IP addresses of both sessions are IP addresses assigned to FortiGate's interfaces.
- C. One session has the proxy flag on, the other one does not.
- D. One of the sessions has the IP address of port2 as the source IP address.

Correct Answer: AD

Question #79

When does a RADIUS server send an Access-Challenge packet?

- A. The server does not have the user credentials yet.
- B. The server requires more information from the user, such as the token code for two-factor authentication.
- C. The user credentials are wrong.
- D. The user account is not found in the server.

Correct Answer: B

Question #80

Examine the following partial outputs from two routing debug commands; then answer the question below.

get router info routing-table database

s 0.0.0.0/0 [20/0] via 10.200.2.254, port2, [10/0] s *> 0.0.0.0/0 [10/0] via 10.200.1.254, port1

get router info routing-table all

s* 0.0.0.0/0 [10/0] via 10.200.1.254, port1

Why the default route using port2 is not displayed in the output of the second command?

    A.   It has a lower priority than the default route using port1.
    B.   It has a higher priority than the default route using port1.
    C.   It has a higher distance than the default route using port1.
    D.   It is disabled in the FortiGate configuration.

Correct Answer: C

Question #81

Examine the following partial outputs from two routing debug commands; then answer the question below.

get router info kernel

tab=254 vf=0 scope=0 type=1 proto=11 prio=0 0.0.0.0/0.0.0.0/0->0.0.0.0/0 pref=0.0.0.0 gwy=10.200.1.254 dev=2(port1) tab=254 vf=0 scope=0 type=1 proto=11 prio=10 0.0.0.0/0.0.0.0/0->0.0.0.0/0 pref=0.0.0.0 gwy=10.200.2.254 dev=3(port2) tab=254 vf=0 scope=253 type=1 proto=2 prio=0 0.0.0.0/0.0.0.0/.->10.0.1.0/24 pref=10.0.1.254 gwy=0.0.0.0 dev=4(port3)

get router info routing-table all

s* 0.0.0.0/0 [10/0] via 10.200.1.254, port1

[10/0] via 10.200.2.254, port2, [10/0]

c 10.0.1.0/24 is directly connected, port3

c 10.200.1.0/24 is directly connected, port1

c 10.200.2.0/24 is directly connected, port2

Which outbound interface or interfaces will be used by this FortiGate to route web traffic from internal users to the Internet?

    A. port1.
    B. port2.
    C. Both port1 and port2.
    D. port3.

Correct Answer: A

Question #82

Examine the following routing table and BGP configuration; then answer the question below.

#get router info routing-table all

* 0.0.0.0/0 [10/0] via 10.200.1.254, port1

C 10.200.1.0/24 is directly connected, port1

S 192.168.0.0/16 [10/0] via 10.200.1.254, port1

show router bgp

config router bgp

set as 65500

set router-id 10.200.1.1

set network-import-check enable

set ebgp-multipath disable

config neighbor

edit "10.200.3.1"

set remote-as 65501

next

end

config network

edit1

The BGP connection is up, but the local peer is NOT advertising the prefix 192.168.1.0/24. Which configuration change will make the local peer advertise this prefix?

- A. Enable the redistribution of connected routers into BGP.
- B. Enable the redistribution of static routers into BGP.
- C. Disable the setting network-import-check.
- D. Enable the setting ebgp-multipath.

Correct Answer: B

Question #83

Four FortiGate devices configured for OSPF connected to the same broadcast domain. The first unit is elected as the designated router. The second unit is elected as the backup designated router. Under normal operation, how many OSPF full adjacencies are formed to each of the other two units?

    A.   1
    B.   2
    C.   3
    D.   4

Correct Answer: B

Question #84

What configuration changes can reduce the memory utilization in a FortiGate? (Choose two.)

    A.   Reduce the session time to live.
    B.   Increase the TCP session timers.
    C.   Increase the FortiGuard cache time to live.
    D.   Reduce the maximum file size to inspect.

Correct Answer: AD

Reference: https://gembuls.wordpress.com/2013/07/03/how-to-avoid-fortigate-entered-conserve-mode/

Question #85

Examine the following traffic log; then answer the question below.
date-20xx-02-01 time=19:52:01 devname=master device_id="xxxxxxx" log_id=0100020007 type=event subtype=system pri critical vd=root service=kernel status=failure msg="NAT port is exhausted."

What does the log mean?

    A. There is not enough available memory in the system to create a new entry in the NAT port table.

    B. The limit for the maximum number of simultaneous sessions sharing the same NAT port has been reached.

    C. FortiGate does not have any available NAT port for a new connection.

    D. The limit for the maximum number of entries in the NAT port table has been reached.

Correct Answer: C

Question #86

Which the following events can trigger the election of a new primary unit in a HA cluster? (Choose two.)

    A.   Primary unit stops sending HA heartbeat keepalives.
    B.   The FortiGuard license for the primary unit is updated.
    C.   One of the monitored interfaces in the primary unit is disconnected.
    D.   A secondary unit is removed from the HA cluster.

Correct Answer: AC